Sports Science

SHAR LEVINE & LESLIE JOHNSTONE

Illustrated by Dave Garbot

Photography by Stephen Ogilvy

Sterling Publishing Co., Inc.
New York

For Lynn Hsu. Thanks for always being there for me. And to Daniel and Kim, two talented athletes—Shar
For Chris, my running partner and chauffeur—L.J.

Acknowledgments
To April Stubbs at Eaglequest Golf Course for her golf expertise. Thanks also to Scott Mackewan at Bicycle Sports Pacific for answering our bicycle questions. And Thanks to Patrick Hespen and Vicki Schultz of Audi AG International for locating and giving permission to use the photo of Ian Thorpe. Thanks also to all our models: Blake, Connor, Danielle, Deborah, Grace, Jacob, Kevin, Matthew, Natalie, Talia, and William.

Project Photography: Stephen Ogilvy
Audi AG International photo of Ian Thorpe, p25, used by permission
Cannondale Bicycle Corp. photo, p28, used by permission: Photo by Kvon
Project Consultant: John Baglio
Design and layout: Judy Morgan
Art Director: Robert Steimle
Editor: Rodman P. Neumann

Library of Congress Cataloging-in-Publication Data

Levine, Shar, 1953-
  Sports science / Shar Levine & Leslie Johnstone.
    p. cm.
  Includes index.
  ISBN 1-4027-1520-X
  1. Science—Experiments—Juvenile literature. 2. Sports—Experiments—Juvenile literature. I. Johnstone, Leslie. II. Title.

Q164.L4753 2006
507'.8—dc22

2005024367

2 4 6 8 10 9 7 5 3 1

Published by Sterling Publishing Co., Inc.
387 Park Avenue South, New York, NY 10016
© 2006 by Shar Levine and Leslie Johnstone
Distributed in Canada by Sterling Publishing
% Canadian Manda Group, 165 Dufferin Street
Toronto, Ontario, Canada M6K 3H6
Distributed in the United Kingdom by GMC Distribution Services,
Castle Place, 166 High Street, Lewes, East Sussex, England BN7 1XU
Distributed in Australia by Capricorn Link (Australia) Pty. Ltd.
P.O. Box 704, Windsor, NSW 2756, Australia

Sterling ISBN-13: 987-1-4027-1520-4
ISBN-10: 1-4027-1520-X

For information about custom editions, special sales, premium and corporate purchases, please contact Sterling Special Sales Department at 800-805-5489 or specialsales@sterlingpub.com.

Contents

Introduction

When you are outside playing ball and someone yells, "Catch!", you don't stop to think about the science involved in that simple movement. You simply take a few steps toward the ball, put out your hand, and place your body in the best position to grab the flying object. Your eyes see how fast the ball is traveling and what direction it is going, and your brain interprets all this information. Your brain then sends messages to your legs to get moving, your hands to stick out, and your eyes to watch the ball. It never occurs to you to mentally calculate that if the ball has a mass of A, is traveling at a velocity of B, with a wind speed of C, it will land a distance of D away from you. In other words, you don't stop what you are doing and take a pencil and a calculator to figure out what you need to do to catch the ball. You just do it.

There's more science in sports than you can possibly imagine. The reason you don't normally think about this science is that much of it comes naturally. But there's always room for improvement, and that's where this book will come in handy. With this book, you will better understand the scientific principles behind sports. You will also learn how professional athletes perform some of their famous moves and why some people do better at certain sports. With practice and over time, you may eventually become good enough to get paid to play your favorite sport.

Obviously, not all kids are interested in every sport. If you live in some place hot, like Texas, the chances are that snowboarding and skiing won't be in your weekend plans. If, on the other hand, you live in Nebraska, surfing won't be high on your list of priorities. However, there is something in this book for every child in every place.

NOTE TO PARENTS AND TEACHERS

This book gives kids a great opportunity to see the connection between science, math, and sports while having fun. Children learn best when they are having a good time. How about showing them the interesting and weird scientific facts behind the activity they are doing? Can you spin faster with your hands outstretched or close to your body? You can also use this book as part of a lesson on physics. In elementary grades, you won't call it physics, but you can still teach the concepts. A fun

activity might be to watch the Summer or Winter Olympics and examine the science involved.

Sadly, many school and after-school sports programs are being cut due to budget restraints as well as lawsuits. You will not need to purchase expensive equipment for most of the activities in this book, nor will you have to drag your class onto a wet field. Kids can learn and master new skills, even in a classroom or indoor gym. It's amazing what you can accomplish with a little bit of sports equipment, and some imagination.

Childhood obesity has reached epidemic proportions in North America. Many kids today spend hours a day indoors, watching TV, playing video games, or using the computer. Gone are the days of a pick-up game of baseball after school in an empty lot. Fine, the empty lots are also gone, but that's beside the point. Generally, children eat more junk food and get less exercise, so many are overweight and in terrible physical condition.

Although this book will not solve the problems of overweight kids, it will offer a

Did You Know?

Children Can Be Champions, Even in the Olympics!

The youngest Winter Olympics competitor was a British figure skater. Cecilia Colledge was 11 years and 74 days old when she finished eighth in the 1932 Winter Games. In 1936, she won a silver medal at age 15.

The youngest Winter Olympics medalist was also a figure skater. In 1964, American skater Scott Allan won a bronze medal—he was 14 years and 363 days old!

healthy alternative to being a couch potato. The activities are designed to be done with limited adult supervision and do not require choosing teams. If kids can become more involved in different sports, then they will be more likely to continue these activities.

A word of advice: Not every child will become a golf pro at 14, a tennis champ at 16, or even a sponsored skateboarder. Don't pressure your child to achieve professional status. Certainly, having a kid who can support you before he or she is out of high school would be nice, but elite athletes aren't born every day. Let your kid have fun, don't yell when he or she misses a shot or drops a ball, and generally make sports a fun time. Skills will follow. Not all kids will be natural athletes, but there's a sport for everyone. If your child does not have great eye-hand coordination but has good balance, try a sport that does not involve balls. Perhaps your child isn't fond of running—try another sport instead. For everybody, there is a sport.

Finally, there's no excuse for rudeness, violence, or rough play in kids' sports. Take time to teach children "polite sports behavior." Set a good example for your children by not suggesting that a referee or umpire is "a moron," "an idiot," or "a jerk."

Teach your child respect for others. Also, most coaches volunteer their time, so make sure you and your child acknowledge or thank them for all their efforts.

SAFETY FIRST!

It's great to have fun and experiment, but there are a few simple rules to follow so you won't hurt yourself or someone else. If you aren't sure whether something is alright to do, ask an adult. An adult supervisor will be able to help you with the activities.

Do's

1. Ask an adult before handling any sports equipment, especially expensive rackets, clubs, bats, or bikes.

2. Always wear appropriate safety equipment, such as helmets or pads, when performing sports activities.
3. Tell an adult if you or anyone else has been hurt.
4. Wear a hat, sunscreen, bug repellent, and appropriate clothing when playing outdoors.
5. Read all steps of any experiment carefully, assemble your equipment, and be sure you know what to do before you begin the experiment.
6. Always leave a safe distance between you and others when performing activities that involve swinging or hitting.
7. Always put away the materials you used during the activities. Don't leave things within the reach of young children.
8. Play only in areas that are safe and approved of by adults.

Don'ts

1. Do not use any sports equipment inside your house. Never swing a bat or club or throw a ball inside.
2. Do not leave a mess on the field. Put away all your garbage, and do not damage the playing area of the field or park.
3. Do not throw balls or swing bats near windows or other places where you can do damage—for example, stay clear of cars.
4. Never make fun of another athlete or be rude to a person supervising a game.

5. Do not perform activities during storms. Come inside and wait until the storm has passed.

MATERIALS

Below are materials and equipment that will be used in many projects. See each project for its particular materials list, and assemble all your materials before you start a project.

▨ balls of various sorts:
- baseball
- basketball
- beach ball (about the size of a soccer ball)
- football
- golf ball
- Ping-Pong™ ball
- soccer ball
- squash ball
- Styrofoam™(or soft rubber) ball about 3 inch (8 cm) diameter
- Superball™
- tennis balls
▨ baseball bat
▨ bathroom scale
▨ batting T (or traffic cone)
▨ brick
▨ bubble wrap
▨ bucket (deep), sink, or bathtub
▨ calculator
▨ clean sand or rice
▨ eggs and egg carton
▨ elastic band
▨ fan
▨ flying disk (aka Frisbee™)
▨ full-length mirror (that can be moved if not across from doorway)
▨ lipstick
▨ masking tape
▨ measuring tape
▨ outdoor thermometer
▨ pan, large (such as a roasting pan)
▨ paper (roll) or paper towels
▨ pen (or pencil)
▨ pie plate (aluminum or other metal)
▨ plastic hangers (three)
▨ record (old 45 or 33 vinyl)
▨ ribbon (several feet)
▨ ruler, 12 inch (30 cm), wooden

▨ scissors
▨ sidewalk chalk
▨ small box or block about 1 inch (2.5 cm) in height
▨ small weight such as a metal washer
▨ spray bottle containing water
▨ stopwatch (or watch with second hand)
▨ string
▨ swivel chair or stool
▨ tape
▨ towelettes
▨ washable marker
▨ wire coat hanger (to bend)
▨ wood (piece of)
▨ yard (meter) stick

Shape Shifters

What does your favorite athlete look like? Is he or she tall or short? Muscular or slim? Broad-shouldered or compact? It all depends on what your favorite sport is. There aren't many jockeys who are 6 feet (183 cm) tall, just as there aren't many basketball players who are shorter than 5 feet (152 cm). Swimmers who specialize in the butterfly stroke will never be mistaken for marathon runners. But what kind of shape are you and what sport do you think you might be best suited for when you grow up?

WHAT YOU NEED

- sidewalk or large area of concrete
- sidewalk chalk
- friend

WHAT YOU DO

1. Lie on a flat area on the concrete, and have a friend use a piece of chalk to trace a line around your body. If you wear tight clothing, like shorts and a T-shirt, it will give you a better tracing of your shape. If you don't have a concrete space where you can do this, you could use a large sheet of paper and a crayon or washable marker instead.

2. Change places and trace a line around your friend's body.
3. Stand back and compare your traced shape to that of your friend's shape. Do the shapes look the same?
4. Ask your parents if you can trace their shapes. How do their shapes compare with yours?

WHAT HAPPENED

You and your friend may have different shapes, and an adult's shape is very different from a child's. Harvard psychologist William H. Sheldon developed a system in the 1940s to classify body types. **Anthropometry** is the study of body shapes and sizes. Body shapes are often lumped into three broad categories. Look carefully at the drawing of your body. Are your hips and shoulders about the same width? If they are, and you have a slender, wiry build, you are probably an **ectomorph.** This body type is often compared to the shape of a pencil, long and narrow and not very curvy. If your hips are wider than your shoulders and you have a curvy rounded shape, you are an **endomorph.** This shape is often described as pear-shaped. The last part of the word, "morph," means

shape, so this is a word that describes body shape. Are your hips narrower than your shoulders? This body type is called a **mesomorph,** and is described as triangle-shaped, with the point of the triangle at the bottom. Mesomorphs tend to have a sturdy athletic build.

People can be one type or a mix of two types, and you can change your body type to some degree with exercise and diet. Each of these shapes is better suited for certain kinds of sports. The good news is that kids are somewhat equal up to a certain age, when it comes to the ability to perform certain activities, so get out there now and do all the sports you can! As you mature and your body grows, you may discover that while you were really good at basketball at the age of 12, you don't have the height to compete with the giants in your class when you are 17. This doesn't mean you can't play basketball. Start a noncompetitive team to play after school.

Did You Know?

You or a coach may discover that your body is ideal for a certain sport. When you are the right age, you can begin to train your muscles to perform certain movements. Adults who are marathon runners, ballerinas, or basketball players are often ectomorphs. Sprinters, or runners who have to go only short distances, soccer players, and tennis stars are frequently mesomorphs. And wrestlers, football linemen, and rugby players are often endomorphs. Besides just looking at shape, it is important to look at the different sizes of athletes.

Jockeys need to be small so that their horses aren't carrying a lot of weight, but a polo player needs to be tall and have long legs to hold onto a horse while hitting a ball. Swimmers who race have huge arms and shoulders, while swimmers who do synchronized water ballet are more petite. In some sports— karate and other martial arts, for example—size and shape don't really matter.

Is There an Advantage in Sports to Being Left-Handed?

Well, it depends on the sport. About one person in ten is left-handed, but this proportion is much greater when looking at professional athletes. Being left-handed seems to be an advantage in certain sports like basketball, boxing, football, fencing (where about a third of the top competitors are left-handed), and table tennis. A major advantage is that the other competitors are not used to having to deal with a left-handed opponent. They expect the ball, sword, or punch to come from a different direction, and when it doesn't, this confuses them. Sports in which athletes don't compete directly with each other, such as diving, cycling, gymnastics, rifle shooting, and weightlifting, don't have any more left-handed competitors than the general population.

Cool Running

When you exercise strenuously, you may find that your shirt is soaking wet and beads of sweat are running down your forehead and arms. No amount of antiperspirant can contain this much moisture. Where did all this moisture come from? It comes from your skin, but how did it get there and what is the reason for this liquid? It doesn't matter what type of sport you are doing—if you are working hard enough you can probably manage to sweat like a pig.

WHAT YOU NEED

■ outdoor thermometer
■ moistened towelettes (the type you get in some fast-food restaurants)
■ elastic band
■ watch

WHAT YOU DO

1. Place the thermometer on a flat surface inside the house or in the shade outdoors. Leave it there for five minutes so that you can measure the air temperature. Read the temperature of the thermometer.

2. Open the package containing the moistened towelette. Wrap the towelette around the bulb or end of the thermometer, and attach it with an elastic band.

3. Blow gently on the towelette for about one minute. Watch what happens to the thermometer reading.

4. Rub the moistened towelette against your hand. Blow gently on the area you just wiped. How does your hand feel?

WHAT HAPPENED

When you blow on the towelette, the thermometer reading goes down. The blowing action caused the alcohol in the towelette to evaporate, or change from a liquid to a gas. The liquid alcohol needs to absorb heat energy to change into alcohol in the gas phase. The energy comes from anything that is in contact with the alcohol—in this case, from the thermometer. When the heat energy leaves the thermometer, it cools it down, giving it a lower temperature reading. The same thing happened when you rubbed the wipe on your hand. As you blew on it, your hand felt cooler. The heat energy from your hand was transferred to the alcohol, which then evaporated, using up the heat.

During exercise, especially in warm weather, your body releases liquid in the form of sweat. It comes from sweat glands in your skin, and is a response to a higher skin temperature. Sweat is mostly water, which evaporates and cools you down in the same way that the alcohol from the wipes cooled the thermometer. Another thing that happens is an increase of blood flow to your skin, which makes you flush or turn red. This also allows the outside air to cool down your blood, because the surface of your body is usually cooler than its inside temperature, which is around 98.6° F, or 37° C.

Did You Know?

People might say that they "sweat like a pig," but pigs don't actually sweat. Instead, they roll around in the mud to cool down. People and horses sweat all over their bodies. Dogs and some other animals, such as rodents and birds, pant, with air passing rapidly over their liquid-coated tongues and nasal passages. Cats lick themselves to make a layer of liquid that can evaporate and cool them down. Some animals, like reptiles, can't cool themselves down at all, so they have to find cool places to hide in when it gets hot outside. In the desert, animals often sleep, hiding in burrows, during the day and come out only at night when it is cooler. Controlling body heat is called **thermoregulation.** In order for animals to survive, they need to be successful at thermoregulation.

Getting Centered

When you play a sport that requires an excellent sense of balance, you very quickly learn a few things about your body. You discover how far you can go in different directions without falling, and whether this is something you enjoy. Try standing on one foot, and then try closing your eyes. Do you fall over right away? Do you find it easier if you really concentrate? Does it help to extend your arms? Is it harder if you tip your head back? Let's look at one aspect of the balancing act.

WHAT YOU NEED

- lipstick
- helper

WHAT YOU DO

1. Kneel on the floor with your behind touching your feet, and place your arms in front of you with your elbows bent. Slide your elbows back until they just touch your knees, and extend your fingers out in front of you.

2. Have a helper place a tube of lipstick on the ground so that it is standing upright just at the end of your index fingers.

3. Straighten up so that you are kneeling but upright. Place both your hands behind your back. Carefully lean forward and try to knock the lipstick over using your nose.

WHAT HAPPENED

Some people can knock over the lipstick, and other people can't. It all has to do with how high your center of gravity is in your body. Your center of gravity is the point in your body where half your weight is above and half is below. Usually women have a lower center of gravity than men, and when they do this experiment, they can knock the lipstick over. This is because women tend to have wider hips and narrower shoulders than men.

Some athletes, such as cyclists, who build up more muscle mass in their legs, also have a lower center of gravity. Bodybuilders or other athletes who develop their upper bodies may have such a high center of gravity that if they were to do this experiment, they would topple over every time. Wrestlers crouch to keep their center of gravity as low as possible so that they aren't as easy to knock over.

Don't Blink or You'll Miss It

Some sports require athletes to have very fast reaction times. Baseball batters need to react quickly to a thrown ball, and sprinters need to push off when the starter gives the signal. Tennis players need to move to the correct area in the court and be ready to return the ball. You can improve your reaction time with practice. Let's see how fast you really are.

WHAT YOU NEED

- 12-inch (30-cm) ruler
- helper

WHAT YOU DO

1. Have your helper hold the ruler by the 12-inch (30-cm) end so that it hangs down vertically toward the ground.
2. Place your thumb and index finger on either side of the ruler at the 0-inch (0-cm) mark. Don't squeeze the ruler—it should be able to move freely through your fingers.

3. Tell your helper to let go of the ruler when he or she is ready, and pinch your fingers together to try to catch it.

4. Read on the ruler the distance the ruler fell. Use the table that follows to determine your reaction time.

WHAT HAPPENED

The ruler fell due to the force of gravity acting on it. You saw your helper let go of the ruler. A nerve impulse went from the sensory nerves, or optic nerves, of your eyes to your brain. Then an area in your brain called the **motor cortex** sent out an electrochemical message. This message traveled along a bundle of nerves in your spine called the **spinal cord.** The message then traveled to motor nerves attached to the muscles in your hand. This caused the muscles to contract, and you gripped the ruler. Using the distance the ruler fell as a guide, you can calculate the time it took for you to respond. Look at the table to see your reaction time. Many things can affect your reaction time. Different people have faster or slower reaction times. Your reaction time can decrease if you are ill or tired. Certain drugs such as alcohol can also decrease your reaction time. Also, your reaction time can change as you get older. Try this experiment several times to see how much you can improve your reaction time with practice.

Distance the Ruler Traveled	Reaction Time
2 inches (5 cm)	0.10 seconds
3 inches (8 cm)	0.12 seconds
4 inches (10 cm)	0.14 seconds
5 inches (13 cm)	0.16 seconds
6 inches (15 cm)	0.18 seconds
7 inches (18 cm)	0.19 seconds
8 inches (20 cm)	0.20 seconds
9 inches (23 cm)	0.21 seconds
10 inches (25 cm)	0.23 seconds
11 inches (28 cm)	0.24 seconds
12 inches (30 cm)	0.25 seconds

The Game's Afoot

There are personality tests. There are tests for your vision. But did you know there are also tests for your feet? The good news is that you don't have to study for this test or take any written exams. Yet you will learn something important about the body part you walk on, which will help you to buy shoes that are better for your specific kind of feet.

WHAT YOU NEED

- roasting pan
- water
- paper or paper towels
- several friends
- bath or hand towel

WHAT YOU DO

1. Place the roasting pan on a flat surface, and fill the pan about one quarter of the way to the top with water.

2. Take off your shoes and socks. Dip your foot into the water so that it is completely wet up to the top of your foot.

3. Take one sheet of paper or toweling, and put it on the ground close to the roaster. Take your right foot out of the water, and press it onto the paper.

4. Take a close look at the shape your foot made on the paper. Have your friends take turns putting their feet into the water and onto the paper. Do their footprints look the same as yours?

5. Try this again using your left foot. Does the pattern look the same as your right foot?

6. Dry your feet with the towel. Before you put your shoes back on your feet, hold the back of the shoes level with your eyes so that you can see the edges of the soles. Is one part of your shoe more worn than the other? Check out the shoes of your family members. What do the heels on their shoes look like?

7. Optional: If you live near a beach, walk barefoot in the sand. How even is your footprint? Do your heels dig into the sand at the same depth? If you don't live near a beach, you could try walking on a large, flat piece of play dough or modeling clay. Just remember to put the clay on a piece of paper and not the rug!

WHAT HAPPENED

You created footprints that showed you the difference between your feet and your friends' feet. If your footprint on the paper or sand was really wide and you couldn't see any spaces under the arch, you probably have a low-arched, flatter foot. Did your footprint show just your toes, the ball of your foot, and your heel, but not much in between? Then you have a high arch. And if you made a print of just about all of your foot, with just a bit missing where your arch curves, then you have a normal arch. If you had four round pads and a funny button shape in the middle, then you are a dog or cat. Just kidding! When you looked at your running shoes, was the rubber worn down more on the inside or outside edge of the shoe? If you tried walking on sand, you may have noticed that one side of your heel went in deeper than the other side. If the outside went in deeper, you probably **supinate,** and if the inside went in deeper, you **overpronate.**

All this information means something when it comes to choosing the right shoe for your foot.

A flatter foot generally means your foot is more likely to overpronate. If your foot had a high arch, then it might mean your foot is supinating. Supination causes your foot to turn so that your weight is mostly on the outside edge of your foot, near your little toes, and pronation causes your foot to turn so that your weight is mostly on the inside edge of your foot, near your big toes. If your footprint looked normal and your shoes show even wearing, then you have a normal foot. What all this means for your feet is that you should choose shoes best designed for your foot type. You should look for a shoe with the same shape as your footprint. Turn the running shoe upside down, and look at the sole. Overpronators should try to find shoes that have straighter bottom shapes and are stiffer, whereas supinators need shoes that are more curved and flexible. People with normal feet can wear semi-curved shoes.

HOW TO BUY A RUNNING SHOE

1. Shop late in the afternoon, because your feet swell up during the day.
2. Wear the same kind of socks you normally do for sports.
3. Have the salesperson measure both of your feet—sometimes feet are different sizes.
4. Don't buy a shoe just because it looks good or because a famous sports personality wears them. Choose the right shoe for your feet.
5. If the shoe doesn't feel comfortable right away, don't buy it. Running shoes should give support for your arches and padding to protect your feet from the pavement. But most importantly, they should be comfortable.

An Intelligent Shoe?

Imagine a running shoe that can sense if you are tired, can tell what kind of surface you are running on, can determine how fast you are going, and can then adjust itself to provide the perfect cushioning to fit these conditions. In 2005 the company Adidas created the first shoe with a microprocessor and motorized cable system. This patented shoe uses a sensor to send information to the computer chip, which then activates the cables to adjust the shoe's firmness. The shoe also has a "brain" that will shut off if the wearer stops running and begins walking for 10 minutes or more. Sadly, the shoe does not have a voice chip that will talk to you and keep you company on long jogs.

Did You Know?

The perfect shoe for a sprinter has only the bare essentials. The shoe needs to be light enough to run in, but sturdy enough to offer support. Elite sprinters use shoes that have spikes, rubber soles, and enough fabric to hold the shoes on their feet. At the University of Calgary, in Alberta, Canada, the Human Performance Lab is researching smaller and lighter-weight shoes. These shoes have a carbon-fiber plate between the sole and the foot. Carbon fiber is a strong, lightweight material commonly used to make sports equipment such as hockey sticks, tennis rackets, and golf clubs. The stiffness of the plate allows the sprinter to have more energy and power when pushing off from the running track, instead of losing energy as heat when the shoe flexes or bends. Using cameras to track the movement of an athlete's feet and legs, the researchers can see exactly what is happening as the sprinter runs. This research has produced new shoes that can improve a sprinter's time by up to 4 percent over traditional track shoes.

Second Skin

Have you ever noticed what athletes wear? Football players wear huge jerseys that cover their padding. Basketball players also wear long, sleeveless jerseys. Baseball players wear shirts and tight pants. Some athletes like sprinters, downhill skiers, and speed skaters wear skin-tight clothes when racing. Not only are the outfits different—the fabrics are too. Sports clothing is often made from synthetic fibers that draw moisture away from the athlete's skin, helping them stay cool and comfortable. Let's see how this works.

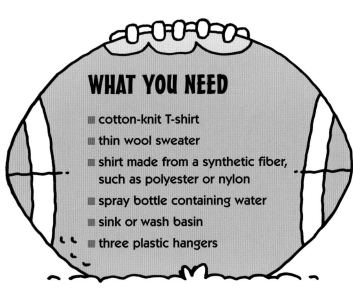

WHAT YOU NEED

- cotton-knit T-shirt
- thin wool sweater
- shirt made from a synthetic fiber, such as polyester or nylon
- spray bottle containing water
- sink or wash basin
- three plastic hangers

WHAT YOU DO

1. On a warm day, go outside into a safe area wearing the cotton T-shirt. Have a friend spray your shirt with ten big squirts of water. How does it feel? Take off the T-shirt and place it on a plastic hanger. Hang up the T-shirt in a shady area or inside to dry.

2. Change into the wool sweater. Again, have a helper spray you with the same number of squirts of water. How does it feel? Hang up the sweater in the same area as the cotton T-shirt.

3. Put on the synthetic fiber shirt. Have a helper squirt your shirt about ten times with water. How does this shirt feel? Hang it up on the third hanger, and allow it to dry with the other shirts. See which shirt dries first, which second, and which third.

WHAT HAPPENED

You probably felt quite cold in the cotton or synthetic shirt when it was wet. Wool clothing has an advantage in that it keeps the heat in even when the wool is damp. This is due to the tiny air pockets that form in the wool that act as an insulator and don't allow the heat to leave your body as easily. The synthetic fiber shirt dried first, the wool one probably dried second, and the cotton one last. This is assuming that the fabrics were all of about the same thickness. The thicker the fabric, the more water it retains and the longer it takes to dry. Cotton is a very absorbent fabric, meaning

that it holds lots of water for its weight; therefore, it takes longer to dry than the synthetic fiber. There are many different types of synthetic fibers. They are made from hydrocarbons, like petroleum and plastics, and have different abilities to absorb water and to act as insulators. Generally, they don't retain as much water as the natural fibers, such as wool and cotton, which is why they are used in athletic clothing.

Did You Know?

Drag is the resistance of an object moving through air or water—it is related to the friction between the object and the fluid. Today, new fibers are used to make clothing for sports that count on speed to determine the winner. Racers want their clothing not to literally drag them down. These fibers are smooth and give the runner very little air resistance. Reducing drag is especially important to competitive swimmers. Anything that can reduce drag as the swimmer moves through the water will produce better times. Swimmers even shave off the hair from their bodies to cut down on drag. Research into swimsuits has improved swimmers' times quite dramatically in recent years. Swimmers help to test the materials and designs of these suits using wind tunnels to show the drag properties of the suits.

One example of a faster swimsuit is the Speedo Fastskin™. This suit mimics the skin of a mako shark. It has small grooves that are like the bumps called denticles in sharkskin. Water moves along the grooves, which reduces drag. Swimmers found that when they used this suit there was so little resistance that it felt peculiar, so scientists reintroduced a small amount of drag in the arms of the suit for the comfort of the swimmers. The suit also compresses the swimmer's muscles, offering support and further reducing drag. The designers used digital images of swimmers and made a three-dimensional pattern to create a perfect fit. In the 2000 Summer Olympics in Sydney, Australia, twenty-eight of the thirty-three Olympic gold medals in swimming were won by athletes wearing these suits.

Several-times world champion, Olympic gold medalist Ian Thorpe tests a new swimsuit design in the Audi wind tunnel in Ingolstadt, Germany.

Scrambled Eggs

No matter how good you think you are at a sport, and even if you have never fallen while skateboarding or while riding your bike, it's important to wear some safety equipment. If you don't believe this, ask an egg.

WHAT YOU NEED

- bubble wrap
- eggs
- egg carton
- towels
- masking tape
- scissors
- lunch-size container of gelatin or pudding (optional)

WHAT YOU DO

1. Wrap an egg with several layers of bubble wrap, and use masking tape to hold the wrap in place. You can make this as large as you like.

2. Cut out one section, or holder, from a cardboard or polystyrene (Styrofoam™) egg carton, and place an egg in it. Use masking tape to close the section and hold the egg inside.

3. If you have a lunch-size container of gelatin or pudding, carefully peel open the container and press an egg into the goop. Reseal the container, and use masking tape to ensure the lid stays closed. Do not eat any gelatin or pudding if the raw egg has touched it.

4. Wrap an egg in a small towel, and use the masking tape to secure the towel.

5. Go outside to a flat spot. Hold each egg in its "helmet" at waist level, and drop each one. Which egg survived the crash? (Don't forget to clean up the mess left from the broken eggs!)

6. Wash your hands after handling the raw eggs.

WHAT HAPPENED

You found a way to drop an egg without breaking it. The bubble wrap was best in protecting the egg from breakage, as the air pockets absorbed some of the force of the fall. The other "helmets" may not have been as effective in keeping you from getting scrambled eggs.

Your head is not as breakable as an egg, but the contents are way more important. Head injuries, formerly called concussions, are now called traumatic brain injury, or TBI. TBI is a leading cause of death in young people. Your brain floats in fluid inside your skull. If you bump your head, even if you don't damage your skull, you can injure your brain as it bangs against the inside of your skull. By absorbing some of the force of the fall, wearing a helmet reduces the amount of damage that will be done to your brain if you hit your head. Helmets also spread the force out over a greater area, reducing the chances of breaking your bony skull. You get only one brain—keep it safe!

Did You Know?

There was a time, not so long ago, when athletes didn't wear protective gear. This meant that they had more injuries when playing sports. Face masks weren't worn by hockey goalies until Jacques Plante wore one in 1959. Players didn't begin to wear helmets in professional hockey until the 1970s, and some players continued to play without them until 1997. Goalie Gary Cheevers encouraged the wearing of face masks when he had stitches drawn on his mask to show where he would have been cut if he hadn't been wearing one. Downhill and slalom racers wear helmets that are designed not only for safety but also for speed. Likewise, racing cyclists have a lighter, but similarly designed, noggin protector. New materials and designs are constantly being developed for use in safety equipment.

Helmets

You would think that one sports helmet is as good as another when it comes to protection. Wrong. While wearing any helmet is better than wearing nothing at all, there are some things you need to know about this vital piece of safety equipment:

1. Don't choose a helmet just because it looks cool. Choose the appropriate helmet for your sport.
2. Make sure the helmet fits you. Don't buy one too big in the hopes you will grow into it.
3. Don't buy a used helmet. Certain helmets are meant to be thrown away if they have protected you from a really hard fall. Hockey helmets are designed to take many hits, whereas bike helmets can crack.
4. While this may be obvious, always fasten the chin strap and make sure it is adjusted properly.

Bicycle riders should always wear the appropriate helmet, as does this rider on a new type of bike that is missing the right fork. This bike is called a "Lefty." The design makes the bike lighter and more stable, because it has less wheel deflection, or wobble. If you think that there's something vaguely familiar about this design, think about fighter jets. The front landing gear on these planes is also one-sided.

How the Ball Bounces

Taking apart sports equipment to see what's inside is interesting, but very expensive. You can't put things back together again and expect them to work. However, there is something you can do to get an idea of what's going on inside a very common type of object. Let's look at balls.

Everyone wants to play soccer, but you only have a volleyball at your house. What do you do? Well, it is bit hard on the ball, but you can probably play soccer with a volleyball if you have to. Most ball sports, however, can't be played very well with the wrong type of ball. You wouldn't want to play basketball with a golf ball, and the reason isn't just the size of the ball. A billiard ball and a tennis ball

are almost the same size, but you definitely wouldn't want to serve with a billiard ball. Gather every ball you can find, and see what gets them bouncing.

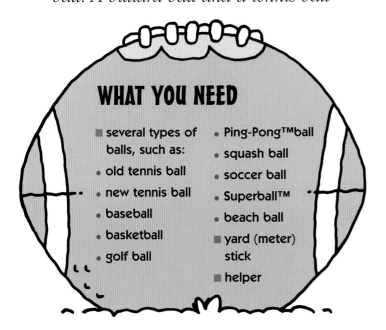

WHAT YOU NEED

- several types of balls, such as:
  - old tennis ball
  - new tennis ball
  - baseball
  - basketball
  - golf ball
  - Ping-Pong™ ball
  - squash ball
  - soccer ball
  - Superball™
  - beach ball
- yard (meter) stick
- helper

A tennis ball, golf ball, and baseball, cut in half.

WHAT YOU DO

1. Find a flat surface to use for testing the balls. A concrete patio or sidewalk works well.

2. Have a helper hold a yard (meter) stick so that the end with the zero rests on the ground and the stick extends vertically.

3. Hold each ball so that the top of the ball is level with the top end of the yard (meter) stick. Then release the balls, one by one, allowing them to drop to the ground. Don't throw the balls—just let them drop.

4. Measure the distance the top of each ball rises above the ground.

5. Try this again, but this time on a flat, grassy surface. Does this make a difference?

6. If you have an outdoor rug, try dropping the balls again. What happens?

7. Try this on a hard dirt or sand surface. How far did the balls bounce now?

WHAT HAPPENED

How much a ball bounces depends on the surface it is bounced on, the temperature of the ball, and the speed the ball is traveling. This also depends on the material from which the ball is made and the way it is constructed. Each ball was designed for a specific

sport. If you tried to hit a basketball with a tennis racket, you would break either the racket or your arm. Superballs™ are too small to dribble and bounce too high and erratically to make an interesting basketball. And you just can't kick a golf ball like you can a soccer ball. Look at the surfaces and materials of the different balls. A golf ball has a tough, plastic surface, so it can survive being hit by a driver. Footballs and basketballs need to have some texture to make them easier to catch.

Did You Know?

Ball Rules

Some ball sports have regulations about the bounciness of the balls used. For example, in basketball, a ball dropped from a height of 6 feet (183 cm) should rebound to a height of between 49 to 54 inches (124 to 137 cm). Tennis balls must rebound to a height of 53 to 58 inches (135 to 147 cm) when dropped from a height of 100 inches (254 cm) onto a concrete slab.

Straighten Up

You would think that kicking a ball straight ahead would be one of the easiest moves in soccer. But you'd be surprised to learn just how difficult this can be. If not kicked correctly, the ball you meant to pass to your teammate can end up traveling in your opponent's direction. What's the secret?

WHAT YOU NEED

- small blow-up beach ball about the size of a soccer ball
- running shoes or soccer boots
- several friends
- backpack or other object at which you can aim
- open space

WHAT YOU DO

1. Place the ball on the ground, and stand behind the ball so that the foot you use to kick is directly behind the ball. Have a friend place a backpack or another object in a direct line from you about 10 feet (3 m) away. This is your "goal."

2. Balance on your other foot, and aiming for the "goal," kick the center of the ball, using only the toe part of your running shoe. Which way did the ball go? Did it hit the backpack?

3. Try this again, but this time use the side of your shoe to kick the ball toward the "goal."

4. Stand back several steps and to one side of the ball. Take a run at the ball, kicking it with the side of your foot along the center part of the ball. Where did the ball go this time? Move the "goal" and try these kicks again.

5. Take a running start, and kick the ball, using the lace part of your shoe on the center part of the ball.

6. Take turns with your friends, and watch closely as they kick the ball. Which method was best for hitting the goal and sending the ball in a straight direction?

WHAT HAPPENED

Kicking a beach ball, you could see which way the ball goes very easily. The ball is lighter and doesn't travel as far or as fast as a soccer ball will when you kick it. Soccer players learn very quickly that if they try kicking the ball with just the toes of their foot, they have no control. The ball tends to go all over the place and rarely in the direction the player intended. Instead, players use the side of the foot, which provides the largest surface contact with the ball. This way, they are more able to control the ball and to send it where they want it to go. There is a downside, though, to using the side of your foot. You can't take as large a swing at the ball with your leg moving sideways as you can if you use your toes. Also, because your leg moves out to the side, you can't use a lot of speed running up to the ball to increase the power of your kick. Using the laces on the top of your shoes allows you to both kick the ball with more power and to have control.

Did You Know?

Air is a **fluid,** a mixture of gases made up of billions and billions of gas particles called **molecules.** These molecules are constantly moving, bouncing off surfaces they encounter. Air can be squeezed and therefore compressed into the shape of any container in which it is placed. It can expand or contract in all directions. Despite the numerous molecules that make up air, it is mostly empty space between the molecules. The air exerts a force, a push or pull on objects, called **air pressure.** Fill your mouth up with air, close your lips, and without swallowing or breathing in, try to make the air in your mouth fit a smaller space. The air pressure inside your mouth won't let you squeeze the air very much. If you squeeze it too much, it will make a *ptttt* sound as it escapes.

Kick Me

What luck! You have control of the soccer ball, and your teammate is in the open, right in front of the net. All you have to do is kick the ball down to the other end of the field. How can science help you get the ball that far?

WHAT YOU NEED

- soccer ball
- running shoes or soccer boots
- several friends of different heights and weights
- two-sided tape
- backpack or another object at which you can aim
- large open space like a field or playground

WHAT YOU DO

1. Place the backpack about 100 feet (30 meters) away from you. This is the "goal."
2. Put the ball down in front of you, and kick the ball in the center of the ball. How far did it go? Did it reach or hit the goal?
3. Try this again, but this time take a few running steps before you hit the ball. Did it go farther this time? Was your aim as accurate?

4. Now do this again, but this time try a new way of kicking the ball. As you run up to the ball, extend your arms to the sides and really stretch your kicking leg, swinging it from the hip, to kick the ball with all your might.

5. Take turns with your friends. Who can kick the ball the farthest?

Did You Know?

When you throw something, the air resists the forward motion of the object. A ball thrown in space would travel a much greater distance than one thrown through the air on earth.

Leonardo da Vinci (1452–1519) was the first person to figure out that air offered resistance because all the air molecules were compressed as they met an object in flight.

WHAT HAPPENED

You probably found that the tallest, heaviest person who ran the fastest made the ball go the greatest distance.

Making a soccer ball move faster is all about **momentum.** The momentum of an object is

its mass multiplied by its **velocity,** or speed. You can't change the mass of the ball, but giving it more momentum makes it travel faster down the field. A bigger soccer player gives the ball more momentum than a smaller player does, because the bigger player's leg has more mass as it swings toward the ball. A longer leg helps because, as the foot swings farther, it hits with more speed. How can a smaller player overcome these advantages? You can't make your leg heavier, but you can make it longer, by stretching and extending your leg as you kick. Holding your arms out at the sides as you kick helps you keep your balance as you stretch out your kicking leg. You can increase the velocity of your leg by running up to the ball as you approach for the kick. If you are already moving when you hit the ball, your foot has a greater velocity.

Fascinating Forces

Another force, besides air pressure, that acts on a thrown object is gravity. In the 1600s, Sir Isaac Newton discovered the force of gravity, that is, the force of attraction between objects. This force is large when the objects are larger, so a massive object like the earth will exert a greater force. When you throw a ball into the air, gravity will pull it back toward the ground.

The resistance an object meets when it moves through the air is called drag. *If you wave the palm of your hand through the air, and then try moving your hand sideways through the air with your palm facing down, you will notice that a larger surface creates more drag. When an object moves through the air, some of the air molecules bump against the object and create* friction, *another force acting on the object. The friction and drag acting on a ball depend on the size and shape of the ball and on surface elements such as stitches, seams, holes, bumps, and the fuzziness of the covering.*

Did You Know?

At sea level, the air pressure is greater, because there is more air above pressing down. If you go to a higher altitude—for instance, if you climb to the top of a mountain—the air pressure is lower. Air pressure is also lower on hot dry days than on cold wet days when the air is denser. Yet, while hot air is less dense than cold air, cold dry air is more dense than wet air. The water molecules that are spread throughout humid air actually weigh less than the oxygen and nitrogen molecules (O_2 and N_2) that make up most of the atmosphere.

Who Sat on Me?

When you think about it, a football is a pretty strange-looking ball. It doesn't have dimples the way a golf ball does. It isn't round like a soccer ball or a volleyball. It doesn't bounce the way a basketball does. And it's not as heavy as a rugby ball. Why does it look like someone sat on it, and what does science have to do with this shape?

WHAT YOU NEED

- football
- baseball
- soccer ball or basketball
- several feet of ribbon
- tape
- scissors
- fan
- adult helper

WHAT YOU DO

1. Cut five strips of ribbon, each about 2 feet (61 cm) long, and tape the ends of the ribbons to one of the pointed ends of the football.

2. Cut five strips of ribbon, each about 2 feet (61 cm) long, and tape the ends of the ribbons to the center of the soccer ball. As the ball is round, it doesn't matter where on the ball you tape the ribbons. (See the photo.)

3. Have an adult turn on a fan. Hold the pointed end of the football with the tape toward the fan.

Where do the ribbons blow when the air from the fan hits the ribbons?

4. Try this again with the other ball. How do the ribbons blow on a round surface?

WHAT HAPPENED

The ribbons on the football followed the shape of the ball and came together at the other pointed end. The ribbons on the round ball went straight out and didn't gather against the other rounded end.

Footballs are shaped this way so that they will travel farther through the air. The point at the front end of the ball allows the air to go around the ball more easily. This tapered shape lets the air go above and below the ball as the ball cuts through the air. The pointed shape at the back of the ball allows the stream of air to rejoin behind the ball. The less turbulence, or air disturbance, behind the ball, the farther it travels. Turbulence causes an area of lower pressure behind the ball, and this low-pressure area slows the ball down. Soccer balls can't be thrown as far as footballs for two reasons—they can't cut through the air, as they have a larger profile at the front, and the turbulence created behind the ball slows them down.

Did You Know?

Aerodynamics is a word that explains how things travel through the air. The "aero" part means having to do with air, and "dynamics" means having to do with movement. So aerodynamics simply means how things move through the air. Airplane manufacturers use the science of aerodynamics. Air can flow in smooth layers with all the air molecules moving in the same direction, as with a stream of water. Air can also move more randomly, as with choppy waves on a lake. When air moves in several different directions at once, it has **turbulence.** If you have traveled by plane through turbulence, you know that it makes the plane bounce around.

Catch!

Does it matter how you throw a football because it has a pointed end? A football's shape gives it certain aerodynamic properties when it is thrown, as you saw in "Who Sat on Me?" But what happens when you don't throw it with the pointy part first?

WHAT YOU NEED

- football
- basketball
- open space like a field or park
- helper

WHAT TO DO

1. Hold a football in the center with your fingers curled up against the laces and the pointed end of the football facing forward. Put your arm back and give the ball a toss. How far did the ball travel? Did it spin or spiral? Have a friend stand where the ball landed. If you can't grip the ball, ask an adult to help you.

2. Try this again, but this time throwing the football sideways. How far did the ball travel this time?

3. Hold the football toward the back pointed end of the ball, and toss the ball so that it wobbles. How far did it go?

4. Try different methods of throwing a basketball overhanded, underhanded, and sideways. Does the ball always roll in the air the same way?

WHAT HAPPENED

The football's shape helps it cut through the air. Depending on how it is thrown, it may spiral, or twist, in the air or wobble. The ball went the greatest distance when it was thrown with the pointed end first. The best way to throw a spiral is to snap your wrist, as if you were shaking a small box to see what is inside, as you throw the ball. This will start the ball spinning, giving it **angular momentum,** and the spinning action helps keep the ball traveling in the right direction. Spinning objects tend to keep spinning in the same direction due to **rotational inertia,** their resistance to changes in spin. So the spinning of the ball helps to keep it from changing position in the air or wobbling. The axis of spin stays pointed in the same direction, as it does with tops and gyroscopes.

The spinning creates less turbulence as the ball moves through the air, and this reduces the drag acting on the ball. If the ball is thrown slightly off its long axis, it wobbles and slows, as a larger surface of the ball is exposed and drag increases. Throwing the ball sideways exposes the largest surface of the ball to the air, and it tends to slow rapidly and drop to the ground. Basketballs don't have a long axis, so they will travel through the air the same way no matter how they are thrown. A basketball can't go nearly as far through the air as a football, because its shape gives it a larger surface presented to the air and makes the air around it much more turbulent.

The Big Show

The pitcher is the person on the baseball team with the most stress. After all, this player is the one everyone watches. A pitcher must have tremendous coordination to control the speed of the ball, the spin put on the ball, and the precise placement of an object thrown at high speed. The pitcher tries to "psych out" the batter by varying the kinds of balls thrown. If that wasn't hard enough, the pitcher must also keep an eye on all the bases and try to prevent an opposing player from stealing a base. What kind of science can there be to holding and throwing a ball? Take a ball for a spin and see for yourself!

WHAT YOU NEED

- Styrofoam™ (or soft rubber) ball about 3 inches (8 cm) in diameter

WHAT YOU DO

1. Hold the ball in your throwing hand so that you have it just touching the tips of your fingers. Raise your hand up to shoulder height with your fingers facing up and your thumb forward. Throw the ball and extend your fingers, as if you were pointing all of them at someone in front of you, so that the ball rolls off your fingertips and spins backward. Watch how the ball moves through the air.

2. Try throwing the ball again, but this time hold it firmly between your thumb and forefinger. As you throw it, give your wrist a twist to the left if you are right-handed or to the right if you are left-handed. Watch which way the ball moves this time.

3. Try throwing the ball by holding it firmly in the palm of your hand. This time, as you throw it, pop your fingers open so that the ball is released with as little spin as possible. What does the ball do this time?

4. Now try throwing the ball underhand. Swing your arm smoothly through, and release the ball when your arm is all the way forward. What happens to the ball?

WHAT HAPPENED

Professional ballplayers don't pitch underhand. The ball can't go as far or as fast. Most kids start out throwing this way, but eventually learn to throw overhand.

When you held the ball with your fingertips, the ball tended to rise and may have traveled farther than with the other throws. This is the way a fastball is thrown. The backspin causes the ball to rise slightly as it slows down near home plate. These balls travel the fastest—more than 100 miles (160 kilometers) per hour. This means that the batter has less than half a second to figure out where the ball is going.

The second way you threw the ball caused it to curve. A professional player throws a curve ball with a snap of the fingers and the elbow, which causes the ball to spin. It makes about 1,800 revolutions per minute (rpm). As the stitches on the ball spin, they decrease the air pressure on one side of the ball, causing it to curve toward that side.

Throwing the ball by popping open your fingers and releasing it with very little spin makes the ball do some interesting things. This technique is used to throw a knuckleball. Knuckleballs are thrown more slowly, around 50 miles (80 kilometers) per hour, and with as little spin as possible, about 40 rpm. The slower speed and spin means there is more drag on the ball. Small differences in the shape of the ball and the slight spinning action moving the position of the stitches cause the ball to move erratically.

Did You Know?

Ball Safety

Throwing certain types of pitches like those described above with a real baseball can be hard on your arm. Pitchers suffer from strain to their elbows and wrists if they don't learn to throw properly. Young players should throw only the pitches their coaches recommend, and most coaches won't let players start to pitch the more demanding types of pitches such as curve balls until the players have finished most of their growing.

In the Zone

Batter up! The batter steps up to the plate. Holding the bat upright, she looks toward the pitcher. The ball is thrown. When the ball is about halfway between the pitcher's mound and the plate, she steps into the pitch. Her body turns toward the plate, she shifts her weight onto her back foot, and then she swings. Her weight shifts forward, and the bat swings across the plate. What happens next depends on whether she hits the ball and, if so, where on the ball she connects. Let's see how to hit a homer.

WHAT YOU NEED

■ batting T
  (or traffic cone)
■ baseball
■ bat
■ washable marker

Boys can be the batter, too!

WHAT YOU DO

1. Place the baseball on the batting T. Use a washable marker to make an "X" on the side of the ball right at the widest point. Carefully line up the bat and hit the ball on the mark. Watch how it travels.

2. Place the baseball back on the batting T. This time, turn the ball so that the mark is slightly above the widest part, by about ½ inch (1 cm). Line up the bat and hit the ball on the mark. Where does it go this time?

3. Put the baseball on the batting T. Turn the ball so that the mark is about ½ inch (1 cm) or so below the widest part of the ball. Use the bat to hit the ball on the mark. How does the ball travel this time?

4. Place the baseball back on the batting T. This time, turn the ball so that the mark is as close to the top of the T as you can make it but where you can still see the mark. Try hitting the ball on the mark. What happens to the ball?

WHAT HAPPENED

When you hit the ball the first time, it moved away from the batting T and probably traveled straight ahead. This is the position in which the ball should be hit to have a line drive, or a straight hit, which may allow you to get on base. When you hit the ball above the center, it probably hit the ground and rolled along—in baseball parlance, this is a grounder. Hitting the ball below center makes a ball go upward slightly and travel the farthest. This is the angle you need to hit a home run. Of course, you also need to hit it really hard with the bat moving as fast as possible. If you hit it even lower on the ball, you probably popped it up and hit a fly ball.

Professional ballplayers can get the bat moving about 70 miles (113 kilometers) per hour in the fraction of a second it takes to swing the bat. When the ball meets the bat, it is compressed, or squished, until the ball has about half its original diameter. The center of cork (see the photo on page 29) compresses, and then expands back, sending the ball flying off of the bat. The ball will travel until the force of gravity brings it back down. The direction the ball travels and the distance it goes depend on the angle the bat makes with the ball and the spin on the ball. Home-run hitters tend to send the ball up higher into the air, making a 35-degree or greater angle with the ground. An earlier swing will send the ball along the line toward first base; a later swing will send it along the line toward third.

Of course, none of this matters if you don't make contact with the ball. And there is no worse sound than the smack the ball makes as it hits the catcher's glove after passing through the strike zone.

Jump to It

Some basketball players seem to stay in the air forever. They seemingly jump over long distances and slam-dunk the ball into the net. Some players even look as if they are running while they are in the air. Does this really make a difference? What goes up must come down. Or must it? Can basketball players somehow change the laws of physics and defy gravity? How high can they jump, and how long can they stay in the air?

WHAT YOU NEED

- flat space or grassy area
- helper
- concrete wall or garage door
- measuring tape
- water

WHAT YOU DO

1. Stand next to an outside concrete wall or garage door, and reach up as high as you can. With your hand wet, mark off how high you could touch.

2. From a standing position, jump up and touch the wall again with a wet hand, making a wet mark. How high did you reach?

3. Try this again, but this time bending your knees and springing up into the air. Did you get higher?
4. Stand several feet back parallel to the wall, and take a few running steps before you jump. Where did you reach?

5. Now stand about ten paces back from the wall. Take a running jump, and see how

high you can reach.
6. Let your friend have a turn. Who could reach higher?

WHAT HAPPENED

When you jumped up, you were able to make a mark on the wall. When you bent your knees, you probably found you could jump higher. When you straightened up, you were able to push harder against the ground, which caused you to go higher. You jumped the highest when you took a running jump. Some of your forward momentum was changed into upward motion.

Your body went up as high as it could before gravity pulled you back down. You and your friend probably could jump around the same height. Most people can't jump up any higher than about 4 feet (122 cm)—in fact, that would be a really high jump. So, if basketball players jump around 3 feet (91 cm) into the air, why do they appear to be hanging there for so long? Well, they are only in the air about nine-tenths of a second.

This is called "hang time." Players who appear to have longer hang times have two tricks. They go up to the top of their jump, and then they wait to release the ball just as they begin to go down. If they pull their legs up slightly during the jump and land in a crouch, they also appear to be in the air for a longer time.

Did You Know?

Naismith—and the Canadian Connection!

The first basketball game ever played was in 1891, when eighteen men lead by Dr. James Naismith, a Canadian teacher, shot a soccer ball through peach baskets nailed to each end of the gallery above the gym at the YMCA in Springfield, Massachusetts. The gallery just happened to be 10 feet (305 cm) high, and Naismith commented that if it had been higher, the hoops might have been 11 feet (335 cm) high. Women took up the game shortly after the men, with the first women playing in bustles, hoop skirts, and high heels. Naismith invented the game in response to a challenge from the school's director, Dr. Luther Glick. He had two weeks to design an indoor game as a distraction for the bored men during the bitterly cold New England winter. He came very close to the deadline, and his game was an instant success.

Ready, Get Set...Go!

Have you ever seen the runners at a track meet getting ready for the starter's signal? If they were sprinters, you may have seen them drop down to the ground to put their feet in starting blocks. They place their hands on the ground and start from a crouching position. Does it make sense that they would start near the ground and have to stand up and run? Why do they do this?

WHAT YOU NEED

- stopwatch or watch with a second hand
- helper to time
- open area to run in, with a wall or curb
- sidewalk chalk

WHAT YOU DO

1. Stand with your heels against a wall or curb. Take as big a step forward as you possibly can.
2. Have a timer tell you when to start, and then run for 10 seconds. Stop when the timer tells you that 10 seconds are up. Turn back toward the wall where you started, and take one big step in that direction (to compensate for the step forward you took in Step 1).

3. Place a chalk mark on the ground at your feet. This mark shows where you would have run to if you started at the wall.

4. Go back to the wall or curb. Crouch down facing away from the wall, and place your feet back against the wall. You are going to be pushing off against the wall when you are ready to run. Place your hands gently on the ground so that you can keep your balance in the crouch.

5. Have a timer tell you when to start, and then run for 10 seconds. Stop when the timer tells you that 10 seconds are up. Look at how far you traveled this time.

WHAT HAPPENED

When you ran the first time, you didn't have anything to push off from except the ground. By pushing against the wall or curb the second time you ran, you had a faster start. Sprinters use starting blocks to allow them to push off with more force. Before there were starting blocks, sprinters used to dig small depressions in the ground with a trowel so that they had something to push off against. The runner's foot pushing backward allows the sprinter's body to move more rapidly forward. This is due to Newton's Third Law of Motion—when an object exerts a force on another object, the second object will exert an equal force in the opposite direction. Your foot exerts a force on the curb, and the curb pushes you forward.

Did You Know?

1968 Olympic Games in Mexico City (the Air up There)

Air pressure affects how fast things travel through the air. When there are fewer air molecules to move out of the way, it is easier to go faster. In 1968, the Olympic Games were held in Mexico City, which is more than a mile above sea level. Athletes preparing for these games trained at their sports at locations with similar altitudes because their bodies needed to become used to the thinner air. In these games, new world records were set in the 100-, 200-, 400-, and 800-meter runs, as well as in the pole vault and the long and triple jumps. On average, runners saw about a 2 percent improvement in their times.

Faster & Faster

Are you a fast runner? Do you like to run long distances? Distance runners tend to be thinner and lighter than sprinters. Sprinters usually have thicker calves and thighs. The bigger leg muscles of sprinters help them go from their starting speed to their top speed quickly. The lighter weight and smaller size of distance runners allow them to use less energy to keep moving over greater distances. How does speed change during a run?

WHAT YOU NEED

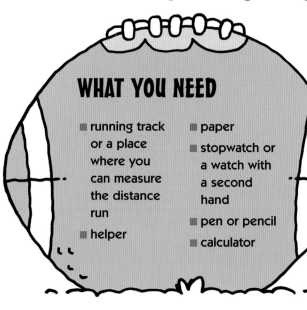

- running track or a place where you can measure the distance run
- helper
- paper
- stopwatch or a watch with a second hand
- pen or pencil
- calculator

WHAT YOU DO

1. Measure off 100 yards (or 100 meters) on a running track. Have a helper time how many seconds it takes you to run this distance. Some running tracks already have this distance measured. Look for white lines on the track.

2. Record the time on a piece of paper.

3. Take a short rest until you feel ready to run again, and measure off another 100 yards or 100 meters so that you have 200. Now run 200 yards (or 200 meters) and have your helper record the time it takes.

4. Repeat Step 3 for 400 yards (or 400 meters) and 800 yards (or 800 meters).

5. Calculate the average speed you ran for each distance. Take the number of yards (meters) you ran each time, and divide this value by the number of seconds it took you to run that distance. For example, if you ran 100 yards in 20 seconds, 100 divided by 20 means that you ran 5 yards per second. Do this same calculation for each distance you ran. This is the average speed you ran in yards (meters) per second. What happened to your average time as the distance increased?

WHAT HAPPENED

Each time you ran a greater distance, your average speed was probably a little bit slower. Moving your body along the track takes energy. Chemical reactions in your body release energy from the food that you eat, and your muscles use this energy to contract. As you run, your body pushes against the air, creating drag. Each time you lift your foot, you are working against gravity. After the initial burst of energy required to start your run, you begin to tire or feel muscle fatigue, and this slows you down. In the presence of oxygen, **glucose** (the sugar that we use as a fuel for our muscles) breaks down to give us water and carbon dioxide gas. This gives our muscle cells the energy they need to contract. The muscles that athletes use are called skeletal muscles, and they contract and bring the bones of your body closer together. You can see this if you bend your arm. Try this: Use the muscles of your arm to bend your arm—this brings the bones of your lower arm closer to the bones of your upper arm.

Your muscles can keep working even if there isn't enough oxygen available. When this happens, the glucose in your blood changes into a chemical called **lactic acid.** As lactic acid builds up in your muscles, this gives you the sensation of muscle fatigue. After you run, you continue to breathe hard until most of the lactic acid is cleared away and turned into carbon dioxide and water.

No Pain, No Gain

Which do you think is the best way to get into shape—running really fast until your muscles burn and your lungs feel like they are going to burst, or jogging slowly for a long period of time? Scientists now think that it's better to build up muscle tone. Your muscles are made up of bundles of different types of muscle fibers. These fibers are similar to long strands of cells all connected together. There are two main types of muscle fibers, called slow twitch and fast twitch. The fast-twitch fibers give athletes a burst of power and are used in high-intensity workouts. Slow-twitch fibers are used for lower-intensity, or endurance, activities.

When you exercise, your body changes the sugar in your bloodstream into lactic acid, a product of the breakdown of glucose. When your muscles have a buildup of lactic acid, you can't continue to exercise at the same level. In fact, the buildup of lactic acid is one of the things that make your muscles hurt the next day. The different types of muscle fibers act differently with lactic acid. Using the fast-twitch fibers causes the lactic acid to form, but slow-twitch fibers don't form lactic acid—in fact, they actually use it up. Athletes can take advantage of this information to build up their slow-twitch fibers by using longer hours of lower-intensity training. Equally or more important in making your muscles hurt the next day are the microscopic tears that form in muscles as a result of training. It is the healing process of these tears that makes you stronger.

Did You Know?

Prosthetics

Athletes who have had a leg amputated have an interesting and effective way of overcoming what would seem to be a disability, or handicap. These athletes have different kinds of limbs they can attach, depending on the kind of sport they are doing. For a sport that requires jumping, they have a leg with a spring mechanism. For tennis, they have a leg with a wider base. And for running, they have another leg attachment. Athletes who cannot walk can ski using a special seat that is attached to a chair on a ski. They wear crutches with smaller ski blades attached and fly down the slopes as gracefully as any other skier.

Love Actually

Tennis balls come in cans, which, when you stop to think about it, is pretty strange. Just about every other type of ball comes in a cardboard container or a bag, so why are tennis balls so special? And are tennis balls only balls with a fuzzy texture?

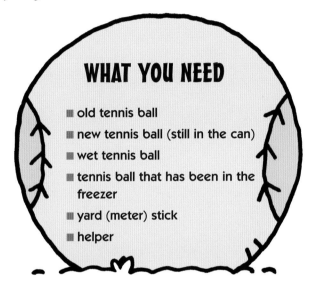

WHAT YOU NEED

- old tennis ball
- new tennis ball (still in the can)
- wet tennis ball
- tennis ball that has been in the freezer
- yard (meter) stick
- helper

WHAT YOU DO

1. Find a flat surface to use for testing the balls. A concrete patio or sidewalk works well.

2. Have a friend help you by holding a yard (meter) stick so that the end with the zero rests on the ground and the stick extends vertically.

3. Hold each ball so that the top of the ball is level with the top end of the yard (meter) stick. Release the ball, allowing it to drop to the ground.

4. Measure the distance the top of each ball rises above the ground.

5. Try this again, but this time on a flat, grassy surface. Does this make a difference?

6. If you have an outdoor rug, try dropping the balls again. What happens?

7. Try this on a hard dirt or sand surface. How far did the balls bounce now?

WHAT HAPPENED

How much a ball bounces depends on the surface it is bounced on, the temperature of the ball, and the speed the ball is traveling. A fuzzy or new tennis ball bounces differently from an old, balding ball. A wet or frozen tennis ball doesn't bounce very much at all. Tennis balls are sold in sealed cans, because the gas inside the ball is under pressure. Once the can is opened, the pressure of the gas inside the ball begins to decrease and eventually the ball becomes slower or "flat." It doesn't become physically flat—it is just called flat. New balls are bouncier because of this compressed gas—when you hit them, you can't deform them, or change their shape, as much. More of the momentum of your swing is transferred to the ball, and the ball is faster when it comes off your racket. There's a very good reason for the fuzz on tennis balls, other than to keep the ball warm (just kidding). The fuzz slows down the ball so that the other player can hit it. When the fuzz gets worn off, the balls tend to travel faster, so players replace their balls every few games. There are even different weights of felt used to make the fuzz, with a denser felt used for asphalt or other hard courts and a finer felt used for clay and grass courts.

Did You Know?

Wimbledon

Tennis can be played on several different types of surfaces, such as asphalt, concrete, clay, and grass. Some players win more games on grass than they do on clay. They find that the speed of the ball and the way they make the ball spin give them an edge over their opponents. One of the most famous tennis tournaments in the world is held each year at the All England Lawn Tennis and Croquet Club in Wimbledon, England. This tournament is played on grass tennis courts and was first held in 1877. About two hundred spectators watched the first year, when only "Gentlemen's" singles were played. The first "Ladies'" singles were played in 1884, and by 1905, players were traveling from all over the world to compete at Wimbledon. Now hundreds of thousands of spectators watch the matches from the stands, and millions more watch the games on television.

That's the Way the Ball Bounces

Thwack! *The racket hits the tennis ball and it goes flying. The ball goes a lot farther than the racket did, and if there were no gravity, it would go even farther. Why is it that the ball travels so far? Why doesn't the ball hitting the racket send your racket flying?*

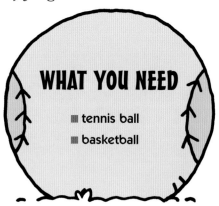

WHAT YOU NEED

- tennis ball
- basketball

WHAT YOU DO

1. Hold the tennis ball in your left hand and the basketball in your right hand. Lift both hands up so that they are at your waist height. Tip your hands, and allow the balls to fall onto the floor and bounce upward. Notice how high they bounce.
2. Place the tennis ball back in your left hand and the basketball in your right hand. Bring your hands together so that the tennis ball is directly underneath the basketball, and adjust the positions of your hands so that you are supporting both balls and the

balls are touching. Let go of both balls so that when they hit the ground, the basketball lands directly on top of the tennis ball. What happens to the balls?

3. Try this again, only this time place the tennis ball on top of the basketball. What happens when they bounce this time?

WHAT HAPPENED

When the balls hit the ground and bounced independently, they both rose into the air, but neither one bounced higher than your waist. Some of the energy of the falling ball goes into changing the shape of the ball and into the sound it makes. The ball has a certain amount of momentum. Remember that momentum is the mass of the ball times its speed. While their speeds are the same after falling the same distance, the momentum of the tennis ball is much less than the momentum of the basketball because it isn't as heavy.

Momentum is transferred from one object to another when the objects collide. When the basketball landed on top of the tennis ball, the momentum of the tennis ball was transferred to the basketball. The tennis ball stopped, and the basketball went a little bit higher than it did when it bounced alone.

On the other hand, when you placed the tennis ball on top, the greater momentum of the basketball allowed the tennis ball to go much higher into the air than when it bounced by itself. When you play tennis, the momentum of the racket is greater than that of the ball, so the ball travels much faster after you hit it than it did before.

Did You Know?

Tennis Courts

How do you make a tennis court? That depends on the type of court and the location of the court. Concrete and asphalt courts are the most durable and require the least maintenance. Clay courts and grass courts must be watered, compacted with heavy rollers, and kept swept or cut. The grass courts tend to be the fastest surfaces, and the clay courts the slowest. Both are gentler on your knees and hips as you move back and forth during play. To make a court, the builders dig down about 2 feet (60 cm)and make sure that this is compacted solidly. Then base layers of rocks and gravel are added and compacted. Finally, the surface layers are applied. In the past, builders used strings with levels, but now they are more likely to use lasers to level the surface. These narrow intense beams reveal the high and low spots. When the court is level, the lines are painted on.

Half Pipe

When you are walking and you want to turn right, you simply turn your body, point your feet in that direction, and there you go. Likewise, when you want to go left, it's a simple action. If you were riding a bike, you would turn the handlebars the direction you wanted to take and lean your body slightly into the turn. But what happens when your feet aren't on the ground? Do you do the same thing as when you are walking? And just how would you turn in the middle of the air? This isn't something that you have to do every day, but if you were in a half pipe on a snowboard or even a skateboard, this is something that you really would need to master.

WHAT YOU NEED

■ swivel chair

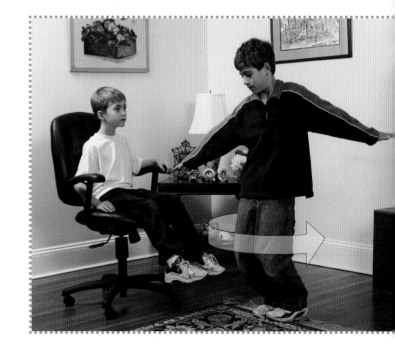

WHAT YOU DO

1. Stand straight with your legs together and your arms out. Jump in the air and try to turn left. Now do this again and try to turn right. You probably went about a quarter turn in that direction.

2. Sit in the swivel chair, and raise your feet so that they don't touch the ground. Hold your hands out, and place your feet straight out, even with your knees. Move your hands and try to move your body. In which direction did you turn?

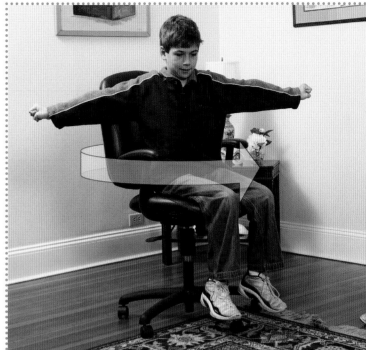

WHAT HAPPENED

Your body turned in the opposite direction to the direction of your arms. As we saw in "Ready, Get Set...Go!" (page 51), objects obey Newton's Third Law. This is the law that states that when an object exerts a force, an equal and opposite force is exerted on the object.
You move your arms one way, and the rest of your body moves the other way to compensate. Why is this important to skateboarders and

snowboarders? An athlete going down one side of the half pipe to the other doesn't aim straight across the hill. Instead, the athlete angles his or her board. If boarders just moved their arms to turn, their legs would go the opposite way and they wouldn't make the turn. Instead, they go up to the top of the half pipe, and they push the edge of their board against the snow or other material. The snow or the edge of the half pipe pushes back, and this allows them to make the turn or spin.

Did You Know?

Swing Like a Pendulum

How is a boarder in a half pipe like a pendulum on the end of a string? They both change energy from potential, or stored, energy to **kinetic energy,** the energy of motion. This transformation of energy from one type to another and back again illustrates how energy is conserved (not used up), but rather changed into different forms of energy. At the top of the half pipe, the boarders stop moving and have only **potential energy.** As they slide downhill, their potential energy changes to kinetic energy and they pick up speed. At the bottom of the hill, they are traveling the fastest and they have only kinetic energy. They move up the other side of the half pipe, slowing down and changing the kinetic energy back into potential. Eventually, they stop at the top again, and the pattern repeats itself. But friction also uses up some of the energy so they have to give a little extra effort.

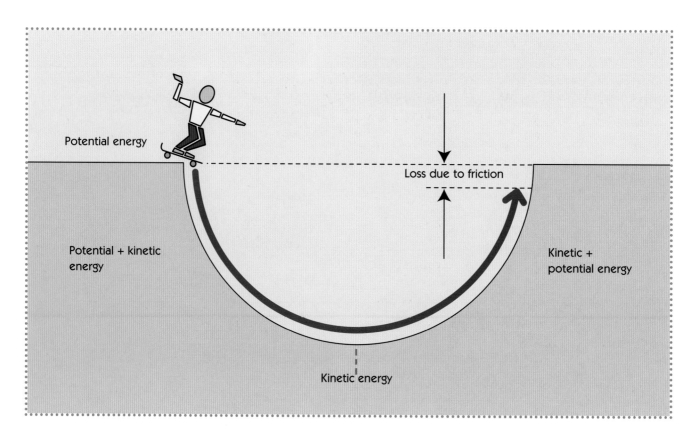

Potential energy

Loss due to friction

Potential + kinetic energy

Kinetic + potential energy

Kinetic energy

Weight for Me, Please

When you are cruising along on a skateboard, surfing the waves, or flying down the slopes on skis or a snowboard, you begin to realize the importance of weighting and unweighting.

Now that's probably something that the average kid doesn't think about much, but you do this unconsciously every time you jump up and down.

WHAT YOU NEED

- bathroom scale
- helper

WHAT YOU DO

1. Place the bathroom scale in the middle of the room on a tile or wooden floor.

2. Stand on the scale with your feet a little apart and your hands straight out beside you.

3. Lean slightly to the left, transferring all your weight to your left foot, and lift your right foot just a little off the scale. Have your friend watch the scale readings closely.

4. Now slowly put your right foot down, while gently taking the weight off your left foot. You should feel a rocking motion as you do this. What happens to your weight on the scale as you shift your weight from left to right and from right to left?

5. Now stand with your legs together and bend your knees. Watch the scale closely as you stand straight up.

6. Turn sideways so that both your feet go across the scale, and shift your weight from the balls of your feet to your heels. How did the scale change when you did this?

WHAT HAPPENED

You're skiing. That up-and-down weighting-and-unweighting motion is what skiers, surfers, and skateboarders use to turn. When you bent your knees and stood up fast, the scale showed that you weighed less, even though your actual weight didn't change. The scale will even change a little when you rock from side to side. When skiing, the unweighting makes it easier to turn your skis. For a fraction of a second, you don't weigh as much, so there is less downward force acting on the ski. The ski becomes easier to turn without the added weight and friction.

If you have a second scale handy, try this again with one foot on each scale.

Did You Know?

Weight vs. Mass

The bathroom scale measured your weight. Your weight depends on two things: your mass and the force of gravity. But aren't they the same thing? No, your mass is always the same, no matter where you go, but your weight depends on gravity. Can gravity change? Yes, but not very much, unless you go some place with much less gravity than the earth. On the moon you would weigh about one-sixth your earth weight. Mass is measured using a balance, which compares the mass of an object (like you) to the mass of a standard, and will give the same reading in any type of gravity.

Stuck in the Middle with You

If you watch the Olympic Games, you have probably seen gymnasts competing on the balance beam. This slightly padded beam is only about 4 inches (10 cm) wide and is 5 ½ feet (168 cm) off the ground. The gymnasts walk, run, leap, and turn on the beam. They also do aerial moves, such as back handsprings and somersaults, high in the air above the beam. All of these moves require a good sense of timing and a perfect sense of balance. Whenever the gymnast poses on the beam, she must keep her center of gravity over the beam to avoid a tumble.

WHAT YOU NEED

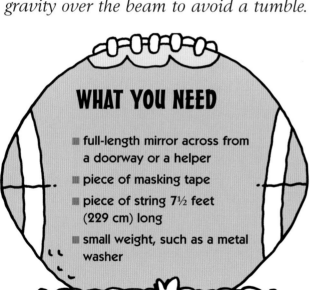

- full-length mirror across from a doorway or a helper
- piece of masking tape
- piece of string 7½ feet (229 cm) long
- small weight, such as a metal washer

WHAT YOU DO

1. Attach a small weight to one end of a piece of string. Ask an adult to tape the other end of the string in the middle of the trim above the door opening so that the string hangs down in the middle of the doorway.

2. Stand behind the doorway, looking through toward the mirror, with your feet about 6 inches (15 cm) apart, with one foot on each side of the string. Look at yourself in the mirror, or have a helper stand in front of you and look at you. Half of your body should be on each side of the string.

3. Lift your left arm, and point your left hand away from your body. Look in the mirror—where is the rest of your body relative to the string?
4. Lift your left leg out to the side of your body, as high in the air as you can balance. Look in the mirror—where is the rest of your body relative to the string?

WHAT HAPPENED

When you stood on both feet and looked at the mirror, the string was right in front of the center of your body. You lifted your arm and, in order to keep your balance, you probably shifted your body slightly to the left. When you lifted your right leg, you needed to shift your body to the left or you would have fallen over. You needed to keep your center of gravity over your feet in order to stay standing. If you watch gymnasts posing on the balance beam, you will see that if they are standing with one leg raised, the rest of their body leans in the opposite direction, just as yours did.

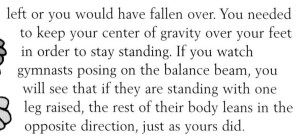

Did You Know?

Never Say Diet!

Elite gymnasts have several similarities in body type. Girls who excel at gymnastics tend to have smaller bodies and are very strong for their weight. They also often have shorter arms and legs, broad shoulders, and narrow hips. But anyone can do gymnastics, and athletes with any body type will benefit from the increased strength and coordination that gymnastics training provides. To be strong, you need to make sure that you eat enough protein, fat, and carbohydrates and that you drink enough water. For growing gymnasts, dieting is simply not an option. A poor diet won't give you enough energy to compete and can cause the loss of muscle, which is essential to peak performance. Eating some time before exercising (but not right before) is essential to provide fuel for your muscles. Snacks and frequent sips of water while exercising are also good for keeping up your strength.

Different Strokes

Take your hand and fan your face by waving your hand back and forth. Can you feel the cool breeze created by the movement of your hand? The way you hold your hand and place your fingers changes the amount of air you push over your face. For swimmers, holding their hands in the correct position and moving them in a precise pattern will affect the way they push through the water. Here's a way to see how water is pushed around by something as small as the palm of your hand.

WHAT YOU NEED

■ small portable fan
■ adult helper

WHAT YOU DO

1. Have an adult turn on a fan. Move far enough away from the fan that you cannot touch it.

2. Spread your fingers and hold them in front of the fan. Move your hand back and forth, and feel the movement of the air through your fingers.

3. Do this again, but this time closing your fingers and cupping your hand. How does the air feel this time?

4. The next time you go swimming, try using different kinds of strokes with your fingers. Try moving the water with your fingers open and then with your fingers closed and hands cupped. Can you feel a difference?

WHAT HAPPENED

When you cupped your hand, you felt more force than if the fluid were allowed to go around your fingers. Swimmers cup their hands as they swim so that their hands act as paddles to push the water backward and the swimmer forward. When swimming freestyle, the swimmer's hands make an "S" shape as they propel the swimmer through the water. The edge of each hand cuts through the water with some water moving under and some over the hand. The water under the hand moves faster, and this causes **lift,** which moves the swimmer forward. Changing the angle at which the hand cuts through the water allows the swimmer to adjust the amount of lift to increase speed.

Buoyancy

Are you a sinker or a floater? Some people are really good at sinking—they can sit on the bottom of the pool and watch the action above them. Other people can float at the top seemingly without effort. Can sinkers float? Can floaters sink? What allows us to change our natural buoyancy?

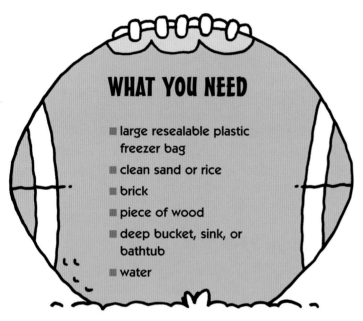

WHAT YOU NEED

- large resealable plastic freezer bag
- clean sand or rice
- brick
- piece of wood
- deep bucket, sink, or bathtub
- water

WHAT YOU DO

1. Fill a deep bucket, sink, or bathtub about three-quarters full with water.
2. Carefully place a brick into the water. What happens?
3. Place a piece of wood into the water. What do you see?

4. Pour about ½ cup (125 mL) of clean sand or rice into the freezer bag, press out all the air, and seal it closed. Place the bag into the water. What happens?

5. Open the freezer bag. Carefully blow air into the bag, being cautious about swallowing any sand (or rice). When the bag is full of air, seal it up. Place the bag in the water. What do you see?

WHAT HAPPENED

The brick sank to the bottom of the container, but the block of wood floated. This is because the wood is less dense than the water and the brick is denser than the water. **Density** is a measure of the amount of mass that an object has for each unit of its volume. When you placed sand into the bag, you found that it sank in the water. Adding air allowed the bag and the sand to float. The extra air didn't increase the mass of the bag by very much, but it greatly increased its volume. This increase in volume caused the bag to have a much lower density, and when the density was less than that of the water, the bag floated.

What does this have to do with swimming and other water sports? Swimmers decrease their density by filling their lungs with air, just as you did with the freezer bag.

Did You Know?

"Scuba" stands for Self-Contained Underwater Breathing Apparatus and refers to the tanks that scuba divers wear when they are deep under the surface of the water. In addition to wearing tanks with air to breathe, divers also wear two types of devices to control their buoyancy. Divers wear weights made of a dense material, such as the metal lead, to make them heavier so that they will sink.

They also wear a piece of vest-like equipment called a Buoyancy Compensator, or BC. The BC has chambers that the diver can fill with air. Adjusting the amount of air in the BC allows divers to move up and down and to return safely to the surface.

Take a Deep Breath

Swimming is a great form of exercise that just about everyone can learn to enjoy. Of course, you can't breathe underwater unless you are wearing some type of equipment. But what do your lungs have to do with your ability to swim? The way you kick your legs and move your hands has a great deal to do with the physics of moving through the water, but what about the way you hold your breath?

WHAT YOU NEED

- stopwatch
- helper

WHAT YOU DO

1. Take a deep breath and hold your breath. Let out all your air at once when you can no longer hold your breath. Have a friend use a stopwatch to time how long you can hold your breath.

2. Take several deep breaths, and then take one huge breath and hold it. Have your friend time you again. Did you hold your breath longer?

3. Repeat Step 2, but this time instead of letting the air out of your lungs all at once, slowly breathe out through your nose. How long did it take this time before you needed a breath?

WHAT HAPPENED

You were able to hold your breath longer when you took a few deep breaths first. Every time you breathe, your lungs are exchanging oxygen in the air with carbon dioxide, a waste product of your respiration. By taking several deep breaths close together, you are making sure that you have lots of oxygen in your blood to begin with. When the level of carbon dioxide in your blood gets too high, your body tries to breathe. Swimmers need to have a large lung capacity to swim long distances underwater. The longer swimmers can hold their breath, the less energy they need to use when taking a breath. Swimmers learn to coordinate their breathing and swimming stroke to move smoothly through the water at the greatest speed possible.

Did You Know?

Synchronized swimming looks effortless as seen on television or from the stands, but it is a very demanding sport. Not only are you twisting, lifting, and turning your body, but you are also doing it underwater, unable to breathe for a few minutes at a time! Your body reacts in an interesting way to this lack of air. When your body detects the lower amount of oxygen in your blood, your heart rate slows slightly. Then, when you breathe, your heart speeds up. When swimmers are competing, their hearts can slow to 120 beats per minute and then soar to 200 beats per minute and then fall again. The times when the heart is beating slower allow the swimmers to keep going. Experienced synchro swimmers practice and learn to pace themselves so that they can keep up with the rest of the team.

Ultimate UFO

Usually you play sports with other people, but here's one of the few sports you can play with an animal. No, you don't need a horse. You can use a dog . . . or another friend if you haven't got a large dog. It should also be noted that a dog will not be using any mathematics to calculate how fast the object is flying and the effect of wind speed or disk angle or other physics. Your mutt will simply catch and fetch.

WHAT YOU NEED

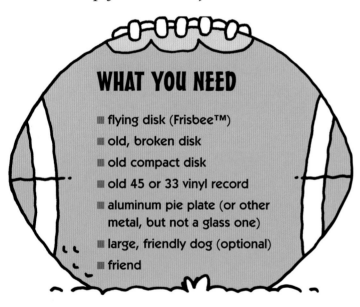

- flying disk (Frisbee™)
- old, broken disk
- old compact disk
- old 45 or 33 vinyl record
- aluminum pie plate (or other metal, but not a glass one)
- large, friendly dog (optional)
- friend

WHAT YOU DO

1. Stand and hold the disk inward toward your body with your arm cradling the disk, and then snap your wrist away from you. Try to keep the disk flat when you are throwing it. Aim toward your friend or a dog that wants to play catch. (If you are right-handed, the disk will be rotating in a clockwise direction.)

2. When the disk comes back to you, throw it again, but this time holding your arm out and away from your body, keeping the disk as flat as possible. The disk should now be traveling in a counterclockwise direction.

3. Try throwing the disk again, but this time at an angle.

4. Let's get moving. Try throwing it again, only this time while you are running. Can you accurately aim the disk in the direction and toward the place that you want it to land?

5. What happens when you launch the disk at different heights? Is it easier to throw it from waist level or from shoulder level? Where are your launches most accurate?

6. Try using other disk-shaped objects instead of the Frisbee. What happens when you throw them? Do they behave differently?

WHAT HAPPENED

The way you threw the flying disk affected the distance it flew, the direction, and its speed. Although you can't see it, there's air flowing over and below the object as it sails through the air. When you held the disk inward, toward your body with your arm cradling it, and then snapped your wrist away from you, the disk went farther than when you held your arm out and the disk away from you. As with throwing a football, you don't want the Frisbee to wobble in the air. It will travel farther and faster if it is level. The Frisbee needs to spin fast enough to travel forward or to turn. The shape of the disk allows the air to be trapped underneath it and to travel more slowly than the air above it. The faster moving air over the top has less air pressure than the slower air underneath. This gives the disk lift. As for the other objects, the flat records or CDs didn't travel very far, because they couldn't slow the air underneath. The surface of the broken disk also cut down on the distance it could travel. However, an inverted pie plate did manage to get off the ground, so to speak. Look at the shape of the pie plate, and you will see the inspiration for this object.

Did You Know?

Flying disks have been around since the ancient Greeks competed in discus-throwing in the early Olympic games. However, the Frisbee has a more recent origin. A bakery near Yale University called the Frisbie Pie Company made pies and cookies that were purchased by students. The pie pans, with a distinctive Frisbie label, were probably the first Frisbees, as students tossed them around. The first plastic disks were made by American inventors Fred Morrison and Warren Franscioni, who made injection-molded plastic disks in the late 1940s. The disks went into widespread production in the late 1950s and were then renamed "Frisbees." Ultimate Frisbee was invented by a group of high school students in 1967, in Maplewood, New Jersey. A newer Frisbee game, Frisbee golf, invented in the late 1970s, is played by millions of people on playing courses with special golfing disks.

Ultimate Frisbee

Have you tried Ultimate? This new sport is certainly the ultimate in fun. Two teams of seven players each try to pass a flying disk down the field until it is caught in the end zone. Players try to intercept or block the disk as the other team throws it. Each team calls its own penalties and the players can hold onto the disk only for a count of ten.

This exciting new non-contact sport is best described as a cross between soccer and football.

Glossary

aerobic respiration The use of glucose and oxygen to create energy in the cells of living things. Low-intensity long-duration activities like jogging, biking, walking, and rollerblading can be aerobic activities. If you can continue doing an activity without getting out of breath, you are using aerobic respiration.

aerodynamics The science that deals with air in motion and the forces that both cause that motion and are caused by it.

air resistance The slowing effect on an object moving through the air caused by rubbing against molecules of air.

anaerobic respiration The creation of energy in the cells of living things that does not use oxygen. Anaerobic activities like weightlifting and sprinting are too fast and intense for cells to get the oxygen they need. Lactic acid, a waste product of anaerobic respiration, causes a burning sensation in muscles.

angular momentum The strength of a spinning motion.

It is calculated by multiplying together a spinning object's velocity and mass times a number describing how its mass is distributed.

anthropometry The study of body shape and sizes.

carbon dioxide Colorless, odorless gas. It is the waste product that living things produce when they combine sugar with oxygen to release energy.

center of mass The point at which all the mass of an object can be thought to be concentrated. If an object were hung from its center of mass, it would be in balance. Same as *center of gravity*.

conservation of momentum A law that says that when two or more objects collide, the total momentum of the objects before the collision is the same as the total momentum of the objects after the collision. The total momentum remains constant and is only changed through action of a force as described by Newton's laws of motion (*see* Newton's Three Laws).

deionized water Water from which all dissolved salts have been removed. **density** The measure of the "compactness" of an object. It is determined by dividing an object's mass by its volume. Water has a density of 1 gram per cubic centimeter (g/cc). Anything with a density greater than 1 g/cc sinks; anything with a lower density floats in water.

drag *See* air resistance.

ectomorph Body shape in which your shoulders and waist are about the same width.

electrolytes Salts in your body that help muscles to contract and nerve impulses to travel.

endomorph Body shape in which your waist is wider than your shoulders.

fluid A substance that can flow. Liquids and gases are both considered fluids.

friction A force that goes against the motion of an object. Friction is caused by the rubbing of one substance against another. It can be caused by a solid (e.g., running shoes on a track), liquid (e.g., water resistance against a swimmer), or gas (e.g., air resistance on a football).

glucose A simple form of sugar. It is the most basic fuel for all cells in most living things.

kinetic energy The energy of moving objects.

lactic acid A waste product of anaerobic respiration. It builds up in muscles as a result of sprints and other high-intensity exercises. It causes the burning sensation in affected muscles.

lift The force causing an upward motion of an object through air or water.

mass The amount of matter in an object. Unlike weight, mass is measured by a balance and is not affected by gravity.

mesomorph Body shape in which your shoulders are wider than your waist.

momentum The strength of a motion. Momentum is determined by multiplying the mass of an object by its velocity.

motor cortex The part of your brain that controls how you move your body.

Newton's Three Laws The First Law of Motion is often called the "Law of Inertia," stating that an object in motion tends to remain in motion unless a force is applied. The Second Law states that a force applied to a mass causes a *change in velocity* (an acceleration). The Third Law states that for every action there is an equal and opposite reaction.

potential energy The energy of an object based on position. If you dropped one tennis ball from shoulder height and one from waist height, the one from shoulder height would start off with more potential energy.

rotational inertia An object's resistance to changes in spin. An object with a high rotational inertia would be difficult to start spinning and difficult to stop once it got going. The mass of an object and its radius determine its rotational inertia (also called "moment of inertia"). For example, a bike training wheel

has less rotational inertia than a regular bike wheel because it is both smaller and lighter.

spinal cord A large bundle of nerve fibers that runs through your spine.

thermoregulation The process of controlling one's body temperature.

turbulence The chaotic, swirling motion of a fluid (like water or air).

velocity Another word for speed. The distance traveled divided by the time it takes to get there gives an object's velocity.

weight The pull of gravity on the mass of an object. The weight of an object would change if that object was brought from the earth to the moon, because the moon has about one-sixth of earth's gravity.

Index